Plastic Is Pants

by Wendy Williams

Second Edition 2022
Printed in the United Kingdom.
ISBN: 978-1-911151-46-3

© All Aboard Learning 2022
All Aboard Learning Ltd, 267 Banbury Road, Oxford OX2 7HT, UK
AllAboardLearning.com
This book is compatible with All Aboard Phonics UK Editions.

All Aboard Phonics Phase 5
Unit 3 Week 22

Week 17	/ai/: <ai> <ay> <a_e> <eigh> <ei>
Week 18	/ee/: <ea> <ee> <e_e> <y> <ey> <ie> <e>
Week 19	/igh/: <igh> <ie> <i_e> <y>
Week 20	/oa/: <oa> <o> <o_e> <oe> <ow>
Week 21	long-/oo/: <oo> <ew> <ou> <u_e> <ue> <u> /oi/: <oy> <oi>
Week 22	short-/oo/: <oul> <oo> <u> /ow/: <ow> <ou>
Week 23	/or/: <or> <ore> <our> <aw> <au> /o/: <a> <o> <au>
Week 24	/er/: <er> <ir> <ur> /ear/: <ear> <eer> <ere>
Week 25	/air/: <air> <are> <ear> /ar/: <ar> <a> <al>

All Aboard Phonics Phase 5
Unit 3 Week 22 (cont'd)

Week 26	Vowels assessment week
Week 27	/ch/: <ch> <tch> /f/: <f> <ff> <ph> /j/: <j> <dge> <g> /k/: <k> <c> <ck>
Week 28	/m/: <m> <mm> <mb> /n/: <n> <nn> <kn> <gn> /ng/ v. /nk/
Week 29	/r/: <r> <rr> <wr> /sh/: <sh> <ch> <ci> <ssi> <ti> /s/: <s> <ss> <sc> <c>
Week 30	/w/: <w> <wh> /v/: <v> <ve>
Week 31	Consonants assessment week

All Aboard Phonics decodable books have a carefully controlled vocabulary and are specifically designed for children who are learning to read and write with All Aboard Phonics, or beginner readers learning at home.

Plastic can be good and us
made is th

ul, but most of the plastic

wn out.

Have you put any rubbish in the bin today? Where will it end up? It will not stay in the bin forever. Heaps full of plastic are piling up around the globe.

Sadly, it can also be found floating around in the water near town rivers, streams and even in the deep seas. You may have seen it wash up on the beach or mud bank.

Land and sea animals can get stuck in rubbish by foot, hoof, head or wing. Stray plastic entraps them and then they cannot escape. When we litter, or factories make too much plastic, animals suffer.

Animals can think the plastic is food when it is in their habitat. If they swallow it, it fills their tummies so they get too full to eat good food. This can lead to tragedy, as some will die from encounters with plastic.

The most helpful thing we can do to save these animals is to clean up the bushes and waterways, and use less plastic. It could take years, but cutting down plastic can have a huge impact.

If you are ready to jump in, look at the way you consume food. Instead of ice cream tubs and plastic spoons, have a cone! That sounds like a crowd-pleasing start, don't you think?

You can also be careful not to drop plastic onto the ground. A bit for you is like a shower of plastic for small critters! So make a vow right now to throw litter in the proper bin.

You could also collect plastic when out and about. If you see litter on the ground, ask a grown-up if you can pick it up. Do it with a friend. You can have a laugh and some fun on a litter hunt together!

Then put the litter int
town. Can you spot t

The sea critters will be happy in the bountiful seas. The birds and other animals that live on the ground will be safer too.

How about we say farewell to plastic?